CHASING STARS
finding
HEAVEN

Seeking Stardom, Finding the Savior:
An Israeli-American Flight Attendant's
Journey to the Messiah

CHERI BEN-DOV WILLIAMS

Chasing Stars, Finding Heaven
Seeking Stardom, Finding the Savior: An Israeli-American
Flight Attendant's Journey to the Messiah

Copyright © 2025 by Cheri Ben-Dov Williams

Published by Dove Ministry Inc.

For information, contact:
Dove Ministry Inc.
www.doveministryfl.com
2637 East Atlantic Boulevard #1073
Pompano Beach, Florida 33062
1-844-777-DOVE
(844) 777-3683

Paperback ISBN: 979-8-218-73565-4

DEDICATION

To Jesus Christ, Yeshua HaMashiach, my personal Lord and Savior. You are the Author of my story and the Redeemer of my soul.

To my beloved husband Matt, my soul mate and greatest encourager. Your love has been a covering through every season.

To my parents, Ruth and Oded, for the gift of a beautiful childhood and the roots that shaped me.

And to the Lewis family: Tandra, dear Nancy (of blessed memory, now home in Heaven), Jerry (of blessed memory), and David. Thank you for leading me to the Lord and surrounding me with love during the silent years. Your faith, care, and prayers changed my life.

Contents

Preface vii

CHAPTER 1
A Star Is Born. 1

CHAPTER 2
The Little Princess of Kfar Shmaryahu 5

CHAPTER 3
Early Encounters with God 9

CHAPTER 4
Shattered Glass. 13

CHAPTER 5
Mom, My Shadow, and My Shield 17

CHAPTER 6
Waves of Youth. 21

CHAPTER 7
Service and Struggle 25

CHAPTER 8
First Love, First Heartbreak 29

CHAPTER 9
Cleared for Takeoff. 33

CHAPTER 10
Grounded, Then Cleared to Fly 37

CHAPTER 11
The Upgrade I Didn't Expect 41

CHAPTER 12
A New Heart, A New Hunger 47

CHAPTER 13
I Gave Up the Stars, But I Found Heaven 51

CHAPTER 14
The Return to My Calling 59

EPILOGUE
The End Is Still Unwritten 63

Prayer of Salvation 67

Scripture References. 69

Photo Album 79

About the Author. 89

About Dove Ministry. 91

PREFACE

This is a story of yearning, surrender, and redemption. I never imagined the path God would lead me on—a childhood of privilege in Israel, followed by the painful divorce of my parents and a move to the U.S. to chase my dreams . . . only to watch them replaced by something far better—finding heaven.

There were twists I never expected. But the biggest surprise of all was meeting Jesus—and discovering the life He had planned for me.

When I surrendered my life to Him, I lost the approval of many. But I found the purpose my soul had longed for. God met me in my pain, healed my heart, and called me to boldly share His love.

In the years that followed, I witnessed miracles, divine appointments, and the unwavering grace of a Savior who never lets go.

If you've ever wondered whether God can use your broken places for something good, the answer is yes.

I pray my testimony stirs your faith and reminds you: "He who has begun a good work in you will complete it until the day of Jesus Christ" (Philippians 1:6b).

Welcome to my journey.

CHAPTER 1

A STAR IS BORN

I was born in the heart of San Francisco, a vibrant, free-spirited place in the late '70s. For my first four years, California was my home, shared with my hippy Israeli parents. Mom was twenty-seven, and Dad was twenty-eight, but in many ways, they were kids, too. I've seen pictures of them from that time. You could see how young and vibrant they were. How liberated and cool.

Maybe they needed that carefree season. My parents were both former Israeli soldiers bound by duty and destiny. My father was never able to shake the trauma of his service during Israel's Yom Kippur War. That horrific 1973 conflict took the lives of 2,656 Israelis, including one of Dad's best friends, who died right in front of him. After the war, Mom told me, the outgoing, funny guy she'd once known was gone. In his place was a quiet soul, introspective and searching for meaning.

My father came from a wealthy family and worked for his father, a strong-willed man who migrated from Poland at sixteen and joined Lehi (the Stern gang), the Jewish underground resisting British rule. He met my grandmother through her father, who hid Lehi fighters. Grandpa often belittled my dad for not being manly enough.

My mom stood in sharp contrast: elegant, determined, and fiercely alive. At first glance, people noticed how petite and pretty she was. But Mom was a little Napoleon, a force to be reckoned with. She was very feisty, a go-getter, and bossy. As a young wife, she was managing my dad. At her urging, my father pursued his business degree at the University of San Francisco. She might have reasoned that a college degree would help Dad find his way. That he'd become more confident or a stronger man. That was the kind of man my mother was attracted to.

As my parents' first and only child, I had a starring role in our family. They treated me like their little princess. Mom always made sure I wore the best little dresses, with my hair and shoes just so. I was her doll, she told me, and she loved to dress me up.

Most of what I know about that era comes from my parents' stories and their snapshots. I do remember that English was my first language, and when we would drive on the highway, anytime we saw McDonald's golden arches, I would say M. I would read all the letters of the alphabet in the elevator, and I would watch *Sesame Street* on TV.

We took long drives in my dad's car, a Nova. I remember being in the back seat, and my mom and dad were in the front playing songs of the '70s. We'd drive for hours while I stared out the window.

But when I was four years old, destiny called us back to Israel—back to our roots. My father could not bear the thought of his little girl growing up without knowing where she came from. And so, we traded the misty fog of San Francisco for the golden light of the Promised Land.

CHAPTER 2

THE LITTLE PRINCESS OF KFAR SHMARYAHU

Our new life in Israel came with a new language, a new landscape, and a new closeness to extended family, but for me, some things hadn't changed at all. I was still the little princess of the family. And, for a while, we did live like royalty.

Immediately after my parents moved us back to Israel, we settled into a small house on the grounds of my grandparents' palatial home in Kfar Shmaryahu, a village that was the Israeli version of Beverly Hills. My grandparents' property was so large that when we arrived, I said, "Nice park." It didn't even occur to me that people lived there.

The home was huge but rarely empty. Family was everywhere—cousins, uncles, aunts, gathering for big, loud Shabbat dinners filled with laughter, food, and stories.

It was an ideal setting for a child. The beach was my backyard. The salty air, my perfume. There were adventures, too. We traveled throughout Europe, staying in luxury hotels. We dressed in the finest and lived a life most could only dream of.

And yet, behind the glamour, there were secrets. Important men in politics often visited my grandfather's grand home—including Yitzhak Shamir, Israel's Prime Minister at the time.

As children, we were taught not to ask questions. Even in a palace, some doors are better left unopened.

At the center of my world was my father. My best friend. I can still remember singing "Strawberry Fields Forever" by his beloved Beatles with him at the beach. Singing along to "Many Rivers to Cross" by Jimmy Cliff on the record player. Watching Dad play with our dog, Linda. My father filled my young life with warmth and made me feel safe. I only wish he had experienced the same sense of well-being. He had returned home to Israel from California, but my dad was still searching for happiness. He was a man trying to find himself in a world that had wounded him.

My grandparents—my dad's parents—were the rock of our family. In the summers, I'd stay at their

London flat while attending summer school, practicing my English. Grandma made sure I was exposed to culture—we saw every Broadway show, ballet, and opera we could, from *Cats* to *Starlight Express*. We'd ride the Underground together. Those were special times.

At home, I took lessons in piano, horseback riding, tap dancing, acting, and more—it was a full schedule of everything I loved.

As dreamlike as those first few years in Israel were for me, I wanted something more, too. A fire was growing inside me—a dream of being on stage, of shining in the lights, of becoming an actress. I imagined my face on a giant billboard someday. I performed in front of the mirror, dreaming of the day the world would know my name.

I was also getting a glimpse of something that would be far more fulfilling than anything fame could deliver.

CHAPTER 3

EARLY ENCOUNTERS
WITH GOD

When I look back at my life, I now recognize a steady stream of "God moments" woven throughout it. These were times when Jesus gently directed my gaze toward Him. The earliest of these moments took place when I was four. After a cat scratched me in the yard, my grandma carefully placed Band-Aids on the back of my hand. They created the shape of a cross. I didn't know what the shape meant, but I couldn't stop staring at it. Somehow, even then, I sensed it held deep meaning.

I was about ten when the next God moment took place. In this case, it was more than a one-time event. That year, my favorite lunchtime cartoon was a Christian animated series called *Superbook,* which told

Bible stories through animated time travel. My parents probably wouldn't have let me watch it, but they were rarely home when I ate lunch. A maid was there to fix me something to eat in front of the TV.

We only had two channels in Israel at the time, and they offered little I'd want to watch at lunchtime. But there was a channel from Lebanon airing *Superbook*. It was kind of blurry and jumpy, but I would watch it almost every day. I remember seeing Jesus in the cartoon and thinking, Who is this? I was being exposed to the New Testament, and no one knew it.

The message behind those stories—the deep love of Jesus—hadn't sunk in yet. In Israel, reminders of God were everywhere. Even the street names in my neighborhood, Bathsheba, Abigail, and King David, were named after people from the Bible. We were taught the Old Testament in school, though it was presented more like literature. But what stood out to me was that God was often angry with the children of Israel. As for my family and friends, Judaism was more about tradition than faith.

Everybody I knew went to temple on Rosh Hashanah (Jewish New Year) to hear the shofar (ram's horn) blowing—part of the traditional celebration of renewal and joy. We were like people in the United

States who enjoyed Christmas traditions but didn't necessarily cherish the reasons behind them.

The same applied to our celebration of the Passover holiday, which calls for eating unleavened bread called matzah. In Israel, you couldn't buy anything made with flour during that seven-day period. I remember Dad and I at the grocery store, spotting a box of cereal we wanted before it was removed from the shelves. The seller winked at Dad and let him buy it. My father didn't mind bending the rules when it came to religious observance.

When I asked Mom who God is, she described him as just a big eye in the sky. I even remember asking her, "Who is Jesus?" She said, "Christians believe the Holy Spirit made Mary pregnant, that Jesus walked on water, and performed miracles. But that's just for them," she told me. "That's not for us."

So by the age of eleven, I was praying to God, but He felt far away. Looking back, I wish I'd felt closer to Him—because one short year later, I needed God more than ever.

CHAPTER 4

SHATTERED GLASS

By the time I was twelve, the little princess had been pushed aside.

My idyllic little world cracked like glass. My parents, the pillars of my life, spoke the unthinkable: divorce. I still remember the room, the air heavy and still. My parents' words pierced through the walls of the peace and security I had known.

Then my father left—and took my heart with him.

Dad's new life began quickly, with a new woman by his side. She was a woman who saw me not as his beloved daughter but as a threat to her place. She seemed determined to pull him away from me, one time going so far as to lie about our dog dying to cut short our time together.

After that incident, when Dad and I talked, she was always present. If I met with him, she would be there. I forgave them, but she seemed to have complete control over him.

It was the same girlfriend, who later became Dad's wife, who encouraged him to start joining her at religious seminars. And slowly but surely, they became religious, orthodox religious. So my secular dad suddenly started to wear a yarmulke, the round, brimless head covering that defines Jewish men. He eventually progressed to a black yarmulke, a sign of deeper orthodoxy, and soon he wore the full attire of ultra-Orthodox tradition. They moved to a very religious neighborhood, and when I would go to visit him, I couldn't enter their apartment because I was wearing just secular clothes, like shorts and a T-shirt. I was just a young girl, thirteen or fourteen, and she would put a plastic bag with clothes for me on the doorknob outside of the apartment. It had an ugly button-up shirt and a stiff, unflattering skirt. I would have to put that on top of me in the hallway before I could even enter their apartment and see them.

I was told, "If you want a relationship with your father, you must be like us."

I couldn't accept it. I knew deep inside that God was real, but this way to Him felt dark, distant, and lifeless.

Even when their rabbi tried to persuade me to honor their wishes, I stood firm: "I don't doubt the Creator exists," I told him. "I doubt your path to Him."

My father and his new wife went on to have new kids. I remember the phone call I got that she was pregnant and how happy they were. I wanted to burst into tears. It felt like the ultimate betrayal: *Now you're going to start making other kids and forget about me.*

And so, a lonely teenage girl drifted farther from her father in a world that seemed increasingly uncertain.

Even before my parents' divorce when I was twelve, the world was becoming a frightening place. The Gulf War between America and Iraq was underway, and Iraq's leader, Saddam Hussein, was threatening to attack Israel with gas bombs.

They would teach us at school what to expect if we were exposed to nerve gas. That nerve gas would make people lose control of their breathing and even their bodies. It was just this dreadful fear that they embedded in us. We would carry a gas mask to school with us. Any time the siren would go off—that sound of the siren was horrific—we'd have to go to what they called the sealed room. Every home had a sealed room with windows covered in plastic to keep out chemical gas if the threat became real. That was right when my parents were getting divorced and separated.

All around me, life was changing, in the world, at school, and at home. My grandfather, who was the rock of the family, developed Alzheimer's disease around that time, and the family business began to falter. Life felt like a castle of sand that was falling apart. Everything was out of control.

My anchor during this time was my brave and beautiful mother. Newly single, she was juggling a career in tourism while raising me.

CHAPTER 5

MOM, MY SHADOW, AND MY SHIELD

My mom was a rock; despite tremendous pressure, she stayed. When I was a kid, she was the free-spirited one, and my dad was there. My mom's therapist at the time of the divorce told her, "Give your daughter to your husband. You can't raise any kids. You're not built for that. You're too much like a child."

And my mom said, "Up to here, I've listened to you for everything, but not without my daughter."

We liked to watch *Not Without My Daughter,* that movie with Sally Field about an American woman forced to flee Iran. It became a reference point for us.

So mom was getting child support, and she was also a working woman. It wasn't easy for her, but she still made sure that we lived in the neighborhood where

I always grew up. We would still go on vacations, too. And because she worked in tourism, we did fun stuff. She would go to these conventions, and she would take me with her to fancy hotels. She took me everywhere, even to coffee shops with her girlfriends. They'd tell her, "You don't have to bring your daughter, you know. We want to introduce you to men." But she wanted me there. I loved being with her.

There were times, even though she had stepped up to make a life for us, when I felt like Mom was more of a big sister than a mother. She was good to me. We loved each other. But I got the sense she wanted, or needed, the freedoms she used to enjoy when she was younger.

She was going through her own turmoil. The divorce process had been drawn out and agonizing: four or five years in court with my dad, his parents, and his new wife. My mom fought them for everything—for finances, for the house she lived in. They would bring a whole row of lawyers, and they had my dad, his new wife, and his parents. Mom would come by herself. She felt like she was David against Goliath, but she prevailed. She was always a fighter.

Meanwhile, the fire inside me for acting never truly died. In fact, as I grew older and my childhood realities radically shifted, the dream only intensified until I felt I had to do something to make it happen.

At seventeen, fueled by determination, I walked straight into the biggest acting/modeling agency I could find—no appointment, no resume—just charisma and a dream. And miraculously, they signed me on the spot.

I had captured their hearts. But dreams need support to fly, and mine was grounded too soon.

For me, the agency was the pathway to everything I thought I wanted. To my mother, my modeling ambitions were a pipe dream. One weekend, Mom was sent on a weekend out-of-town work assignment. She expected me to join her, as always. But this time, I protested; I was waiting for a call from the modeling agency.

She told me, "That's nonsense. These are just dreams. We're going." And so we did.

When we came back, there was a message on the answering machine from the acting/modeling agency. They wanted me to audition for a shampoo commercial, and I missed it. I was so angry, and for years, I felt I could have been discovered, and I'd missed my chance.

CHAPTER 6

WAVES OF YOUTH

Despite the wounds, I found moments of sunshine. Mom and I lived by the beach in the affluent Herzliya Pituach neighborhood, Israel's gem by the sea. I was outgoing, popular, and full of energy—life felt big and bright. I was so thankful to be surrounded by my dear girlfriends, whom I love to this day.

Friends, cafés, movies, the smell of salt in the air—these were my escapes. When I was twelve, I became certified as a scuba diver, and I loved my time in or near the water. All through school, I was part of the acting division and loved every chance to perform. At fourteen, during our junior high graduation, my girlfriend and I stole the show with a clever skit we wrote called *The Snobs*, about two girls who thought they were too good for the party.

What I did not love was school. It bored me; the beach called me louder. I spent many days dreaming with my toes in the sand rather than keeping my head in the books. Scheming ways to cheat on tests with my friends became almost an art form.

"If only you'd use your brains to study instead," my mother joked.

Still, Mom and I continued to deal with challenges. For one thing, finances were tight. Mom wanted me to stay in the same neighborhood I'd grown up in, surrounded by the friends I'd always known, but I started to feel like I didn't measure up financially to them. My friends were really wealthy, and we were "fake wealthy." We had more than enough, but compared to my genuinely wealthy friends, I no longer felt like we were on their level.

Then there were my attempts to learn to drive. They were a disaster, a real-life version of the "Oops, my bad" driving scene from *Clueless*. In Israel, there was no high school driver's ed; you had to take private lessons, and they were costly. I'd ask Mom for money to pay the instructor, and she'd say, "Go to your dad, let him pay for it."

But Dad sent me right back to Mom. She was getting child support, he said, she should be more than capable of paying for my lessons.

By the time my high school graduation was approaching, I still couldn't drive, and my instructor was preparing to sue me for unpaid lessons. Mom had given me money to pay for my graduation certificate and a videotape of the ceremony. (This was before smartphones—if you didn't get a tape, you didn't get a record of the day.) I used that to pay my driving instructor. And at my high school, when a teacher passed out videotapes of our graduation, I didn't get anything.

That was embarrassing, but maybe that lesson in humility served as a bit of preliminary training for what was coming next.

CHAPTER 7

SERVICE AND STRUGGLE

When I was eighteen, Israel demanded its due: mandatory military service.

In high school, I hadn't been a great student because I wanted to have fun. Maybe I'd been a bit rebellious because of the divorce of my parents. In any case, the military didn't base assignments on academic performance. Its IQ and aptitude tests determined that I should be in military intelligence.

I, the princess of Kfar Shmaryahu, struggled with the harsh life of the army. I'd been pampered and protected. During training, people were yelling at me. I had to wake up at 5:00 a.m. Instead of a bedroom with my canopy bed, I was sleeping in barracks. I had to do dishes; I'd never been expected to do the dishes at my house. The others in my unit resented my obvious misery. They didn't say it out loud, but I could feel it: *Who do you think you are? We're all doing this.* The other girls were tough, but that life was not for me.

I encountered the same resentment after completing my three-week training. In intelligence, I was given secretarial tasks. I didn't mind the work, but there was instant tension between me and the other girls assigned there. I was from Herzliya Pituach. To the other girls, that said everything. In their eyes, I was a spoiled snob from the ritzy side of town.

That constant resentment wore on me. I begged the officer in charge of the office to move me somewhere else, but she refused. So what did I do? Exactly what you're *never* supposed to do. I passed over her in the chain of command and went to our captain, her boss. I knocked on his office door and I cried. "I can't be in this office. These girls are mean. Please move me to another office."

He agreed, but he couldn't override the officer in charge of my unit. His instructions to her: "You move her, but you choose where." So she chose the lowest post on the base, where the maintenance soldiers worked, and sent me there.

I remember coming to my office at the base, and my bag was there. They said, "You wanted to move, so you were moved." And they gave me directions to my new office.

It looked like a huge garage. There were doves perched in the rafters, and bird droppings everywhere. Then this girl with orange hair showed up. "Oh yeah, you're with us now. What's up?"

But, in some ways, the new assignment was an improvement over the last one. I was the secretary for the captain in charge. He was so sweet, and he knew I didn't belong in that rough hole. And there was nothing there for me to do. So what ended up happening was I would check in and say, "You need me to do anything today?" And the captain would say, "Nope, you're good."

And so I would call my friend to take me out of the base for lunch, and I would just hang out at the beach and come back. That was OK for a while, but the truth was, I was demoralized. The other girls had written me off as a privileged princess who didn't belong. I felt stuck. Like I was accomplishing nothing, just disappearing. Eventually, I decided I wanted out. That was no small decision. In Israel, if you don't complete your military service, you won't be able to find a job later. It's a black mark on your record. Few people knew what I was thinking, but I did ask a few people at the base for their advice. My options were limited. If I simply left, they told me, I'd be arrested. The only thing I could do was to request a discharge on the grounds that the military was affecting my mental health. But then I'd have an extremely negative mark on my record, one that likely would follow me for life.

I remember telling my mom what I was considering.

"Don't you dare," she told me. "You're almost done with the military. Just finish it out. You don't want that in your file."

She was right, but as far as I was concerned, I couldn't stand my life in the Army. It was wasting my time. Not long after talking to my mom, I went to see the therapist at the base and told her how depressed I was. She released me, and three months shy of completing my required service, my military days were behind me.

I was relieved, but all I could think about was failure. My family had fractured. I had to leave the military early. I hadn't done great in high school. And then there was my complicated relationship with my boyfriend.

CHAPTER 8

FIRST LOVE, FIRST HEARTBREAK

My first boyfriend was a French-Israeli, seven years older than me. A friend introduced us right before the Army, and I fell head over heels for him. It was my French-era consulate classes, a love for the language, and a spontaneous trip to Paris to see my boyfriend, funded by selling Dad's saxophone. He was a party boy—into raves, techno music, and late-night clubs. And he was eager to introduce me to that world.

"You're just living in a bubble," he would say.

I remember during a visit to my mom's house, my boyfriend commented on our indoor Persian cat.

"Let that cat out of the house," he told my mom. "She needs some air. You're trapping that cat like you're trapping your daughter. She needs to see the world. She needs to experience life, and she's in her bubble." So that was his mission.

To him, one of the best ways for me to experience his world was to try ecstasy. I gave in after some initial protests. I'm from Herzliya Pituach; we don't do drugs. "You'll love it," he promised.

And that first time was amazing. The high was really high, and the colors were wonderful. I loved that one experience. Then, a couple of other times, I tried it again, and nothing happened. Later, I heard the term "chasing the dragon." People who had a good experience with a drug want to experience that again, but they don't. So they constantly take more and more because they want to get back to that initial high. But I didn't do that; I didn't get hooked on drugs. It really wasn't my thing. I had one bad experience, very scary, when I lost control of my mind for a minute. That was my wake-up call: that I'm not built for drugs.

My boyfriend continued his mission of introducing me to his world, to adult experiences. And at age twenty, I got pregnant. I wanted to keep the baby. To marry him and build a life together. My boyfriend wanted no such thing.

If I kept the baby, he told me, I would never have him. He would marry someone else and visit his child with her. He pressured me to have an abortion. So did his father. And my mother.

I still held on to hope for marriage and motherhood, and my boyfriend agreed to see a therapist with me. But what seemed like a promising development was ultimately the death of any kind of future together. The therapist made it clear. "If he wanted you, he would have taken you. He doesn't."

With a broken heart, I walked into a private hospital and gave up a piece of my soul. Afterward, I ended the relationship. A love that could not protect me was no love at all.

Sometimes I wonder what might have been. But my story was far from over.

CHAPTER 9

CLEARED FOR TAKEOFF

Just when Israel seemed to close its doors around me, Mom found a newspaper ad that changed everything.

"Hebrew-speaking flight attendants needed. Dual citizenship required."

That was a ray of hope. It was as if the ad had been written just for me.

Maybe I had it rough in Israel, but I could start fresh in the United States. I could picture my first interview.

Wow, you've been in the military? They wouldn't care that I'd left three months early—just the fact that I served would be impressive.

You speak two languages? Wow, that's impressive.

Suddenly, I had a real shot at something bigger. For the first time, I felt like I could actually be somebody.

The airline's application process included job interviews in Israel and the United States. The first round of interviews went well, and for the second, I had the benefit of my mom's experiences in the US. She remembered her transition to life in California and hired an etiquette coach to help me make a good impression in America.

At first, I didn't realize how much I needed his help. But the more he coached me, the more I understood how different American culture really was. My Israeli chutzpah—directness and a no-nonsense attitude—wouldn't necessarily work in my favor in the States. In Israel, if you go to your friend's house, you just open the fridge and help yourself. But in American homes, you wouldn't. You'd ask first.

By the time I landed in Newark, New Jersey, for my final interview, I just knew everything was going to come together. There was something big waiting for me here. And, I was right. I'd have to leave the promised land to have my first meaningful encounter with God. And this job was the momentum that would move me into the arms of the One I had always been seeking.

In America, all I knew was I'd reached my final destination for life. I felt so important, so alive—it was my first time back in America since I was four years old.

I felt an immediate connection to the land, a feeling of destiny stirring.

I passed the final interview and was invited to return to America for six weeks of intense training in Houston, Texas. I packed up and shared a tearful good-bye with my mother. We had no idea that would be the last time I would ever live with her in Israel. I had officially left the nest.

CHAPTER 10

GROUNDED, THEN CLEARED TO FLY

Training in Houston was tougher than I expected. I treated it like an adventure movie, one big party, not realizing the airline's strict expectations.

I faced culture shock, too. In America, you had to be twenty-one to even sit near alcohol. One evening, simple carelessness—sitting next to a drink—got me a harsh warning. I had so much to learn about American rules.

I studied but made a critical mistake: I placed a small Psalms booklet beside my final exam, and even though I never touched it, the airline's HR department accused me of cheating. Devastated, I was expelled from training and sent back to Israel.

But I made a pact with the other flight attendant trainees, now my friends, to return and live with them in a "crash pad" after they graduated. And I couldn't shake the feeling that my heart now belonged in America.

Back in Israel, on the other hand, I didn't feel at home at all. My friends there encouraged me to take a leap of faith and embrace a new life in America. My mother agreed, and soon, I was back, living with my flight attendant friends and working in New York City as an intern for a photography agency.

My new life wasn't exactly going according to plan, but I was loving it, strutting Manhattan streets in my raincoat and go-go boots, hailing yellow taxis. I felt like I was starring in my own movie.

Six months later, the airline called. They'd created a new route from Tel Aviv to Newark and needed more flight attendants who spoke Hebrew. They knew I met their qualifications and offered me a second chance to train with them.

I accepted. And this time, I was determined to succeed.

During my second training, I took everything seriously. There were no more parties, no more distractions. And I needed every ounce of discipline and concentration I could muster for the airline's demanding program. We were taught detailed information about the planes, their exits, their safety equipment, and more. Every afternoon, we were tested on our knowledge. Not everyone passed. But I did. I received my wings, my uniform, and the pride of being a flight attendant. My mom even flew in for my graduation. It felt like the beginning of a glorious new chapter.

CHAPTER 11

THE UPGRADE
I DIDN'T EXPECT

It had been a while since I experienced the God moments that had influenced me as a child and young teen, but during my time in America, there were more of them. In New York, beginning with the office internship I did between airline trainings, I started hearing more and more talk about Jesus.

Well, that's great for Christians, I thought, but it's nonsense. God doesn't have a son. Believing that He did was false religion, paganism. I now believe that God was starting to work on my heart, pulling me closer. And often, when He does that, non-believers' first response is rebellion.

Even while rejecting the idea of Jesus, I found myself drawing Him—sketching Christ on the cross in the margins of my notepad. It was like my hand knew something my mind hadn't accepted yet.

I was thinking about God, the God I'd been taught about, too. I even considered producing a movie called *In the Eyes of God* about how people don't have as much freedom as they think to live a sinful life because God is watching, and how He is displeased. I really gave it a lot of thought. I was going to write the script, and the opening scenes would be in Jerusalem. I would be part of the story, and it would follow my move from Israel to the United States. But I had no intention of including a message of salvation. It would be about an angry God.

So yes, God was very much on my mind by the time I became a flight attendant and started rooming with a Christian colleague. God had prepared my heart and mind for what was to come next: Life with an outspoken roommate and her equally bold mother. Women who seemed to talk about Jesus all the time. My first impression? I liked them, but they were fanatics, just like my dad.

One time at our crash pad, my roommate had a group of Israeli flight attendants all around her. They asked her about her faith in Jesus, and she shared the gospel with them. She told them about Jesus, the Son of God, dying for humanity's sin—sin that separated man from our holy God, leaving man doomed to a future in hell after death. Faith in Jesus and His sacrifice on the cross was the only way to salvation. I also watched the testimony of Kenneth E. Hagin, who described dying and going to hell before being supernaturally healed on John Osteen's show *Beyond the Grave*. It really bothered me because it seemed unfair that you had to know Jesus in order to escape hell. After all, we Jews are the chosen people, right? I tried to shake it off and ignore it, but deep down, I feared that this place called hell was real.

My roommate was so certain that Jesus is real, and that stubborn faith of hers annoyed me. I found myself asking, "What makes you so sure your way is the right way?

"Every religion thinks its way is the right way. We're Jews. We don't believe in Jesus, and that's that."

Then she said something I couldn't really argue with. "Well, how about you ask God Himself if He has a son, and when you hear from Him, you'll know that you know that you've heard from Him. Nobody will be able to take that away from you."

So I asked God more than once if He had a son. I didn't receive an answer.

But then one night, my roommate brought home the movie *Left Behind,* and we watched it. There's a scene where Kirk Cameron's character gives his life to Christ in the bathroom. We said, Wow, he had a revelation of the reality of God.

I felt moved, and I went into the bathroom. "Elohim," I said, calling on the one true God of Israel. "Please, if You have a son, please let me know. I want to know. And if You don't, forgive me for asking."

The times I'd asked God about having a son before, I'd said, "Oh God, if You have a son, let me know." But it wasn't sincere. This time, I sought Him with all my heart, and the Bible says if you seek Him with all your heart, you will find him.

About three days later, I remember sitting in the living room, and I had an encounter with the Holy Spirit. I think we were watching another Christian movie, but we really felt the presence of the Lord. It's not something that everybody has experienced, but we felt a sweet heavenly touch. I felt like the Holy Spirit descended upon me, and I was awakened.

When we accept Christ, the love of God is being poured into our hearts by the Holy Spirit (Romans 5:5). For me, it literally felt that way.

My roommate had a cat at the time, and I didn't like him so much. When that encounter happened, I looked at the cat, and I thought, Wow, I love him. I love her cat. I had the love nature given by the Holy

Spirit. I even remember hearing sounds in the room that you're normally not aware of, sounds that are there all the time. Like white noise from the fridge, but clearer and louder.

And even my sight: I felt like there was a clear sight, like a glow. I can't explain it, but it literally felt like I was being raised from the dead. Like I was awakened. Like I was a new person. The new birth for me was literal. I remember it. There was the Cheri before, and there was the Cheri after. Before, I had been the funny clown, the girl who used humor to hide her hurt.

But suddenly, I found God—not in tradition or religion, but in something real. This was different. This was not of this world. All my God moments leading up to this, the cross bandage that was on my hand, the *Superbook* cartoon, and all these things. I realized, Oh my gosh, Jesus, You were there the whole time.

And I began to really have that one-on-one relationship with God, not through a priest or a preacher or a church, none of that. It was just me and Him in privacy.

I know that when Christian evangelists lead people to salvation, they encourage people to pray what's known as the Sinner's Prayer, to tell Jesus that they believe He died on the cross and was raised again, that they want to turn from their sin and follow Him.

I was born again without saying that. The Bible says if you call on the name of the Lord, you will be saved. And if you seek Him with all your heart, God sees the heart. He's not a God of steps—that's religion. If you really look for Him, he's right there.

That said, my roommate's mom, a Baptist, said, "Make sure you say the Sinner's Prayer," and so I did.

A new journey began. Not just across oceans but into the very heart of God's destiny for my life.

CHAPTER 12

A New Heart,
A New Hunger

After my encounter with Jesus, I was still living between two worlds—the old party lifestyle and the new pull toward holiness. The process of transformation began slowly.

I was still a flight attendant, still smoking cigarettes, still hanging out at clubs. But something had shifted. My spirit no longer felt comfortable in the places I once loved.

I developed an insatiable appetite for the Word of God. In my bedroom, I would flip through the pages of my Old Testament Bible. I would land on something, seemingly accidentally, but I know it was God leading me to these verses. There's a verse that says the Messiah will come out of Bethlehem (Micah 5:2). One about a virgin having a child (Isaiah 7:14) and one that says, "They have pierced my hands and feet" (Psalms 22:16).

Nobody had told me, but now I know there are over three hundred Messianic prophecies that Christ fulfilled. I kept stumbling across them and thinking, *This is Jesus. He was here the whole time.* How come nobody talked about it in Israel? Why don't they teach it?

When I wasn't reading the Bible, I was reading books about the Bible. One that fascinated me was *The Bible Code* by Michael Drosnin. The original Bible was a scroll written mostly in Hebrew, and there were no spaces between the letters. What rabbis found is that with the use of computers, they can track them with Equidistant Letter Sequences (ELSs): words or phrases that appear to be hidden within the text by selecting letters at equal intervals. They can program a computer to pull out a letter every thirty letters, or every three hundred, whatever they want to try, and the letters would form sentences and paragraphs about things that happened in history—and things that were yet to occur, like World War II and the attack on the Twin Towers.

Because I speak Hebrew, I was able to count and see for myself. I thought, wow, this is the word of God. This book stood the test of time.

People have tried to discredit the Bible, but the Bible has always proved those researchers wrong. Before people even knew there were nations like the Hittites and the Amorites, the Bible mentioned them. Then, later, archaeological discoveries confirmed it. The Bible describes the Hebrews' encounter with Egyptian soldiers at the Red Sea millennia ago; archaeologists have found chariots at the bottom of the Red Sea.

There's also another book about the Bible code, written by Yacov Rambsel, a Messianic Jew. He has a book called *His Name is Jesus: The Mysterious Yeshua Codes,* and he found many Messianic prophecies encoded within God's name. Most traditional Jewish scholars won't acknowledge that part, of course, because they reject Jesus as the Messiah. But I was studying about that as well.

Actually, my dad became religious because he and his wife would go to seminars, and they would teach about the Bible code. And when he was confronted with the Bible code, he said there was no way this book was not inspired by God. This was the real deal.

As far as people are concerned in Israel, they believe that if you want to serve God, if you want to know God, there's one way, and it's the religious way. That's what I rebelled against when I was a teenager after my dad became an Orthodox Jew. I said, "God does exist, but this is not the route to him." The problem was, until I found Jesus, I didn't know how to get to Him.

God seemed high in the sky, so far above that I could never reach him.

After I was born again, I realized He 's right here. He's in my heart. He was here the whole time. He is the way, the truth, and the life. That's really true. The only way to the Father is through the Son.

CHAPTER 13

I GAVE UP THE STARS, BUT I FOUND HEAVEN

I was inspired. Exhilarated. Filled with hope about what was to come next.

But not everyone embraced the new Cheri. Friends from my old life didn't understand the change in me. Rumors began to circulate among my family and friends in Israel: "She's in a cult. She's been brainwashed."

People saw me through a lens of my past: "That's the girl whose parents divorced, whose father left her . . . What now?" I no longer belonged to the world they knew. I was born again—made new—and they couldn't recognize me anymore.

I'll never forget meeting a childhood friend at the airport. She had come to greet me on one of my flights. I looked into her eyes, smiling, and at that moment, my heart whispered, "You don't know me." And it was true. I was a stranger to the people I once loved.

Even my closest family members distanced themselves from me as my faith grew. My father had already drifted from my life, but after he heard I had become a Christian, he decided he had a reason to disappear completely. My mother tried to maintain contact, but our relationship grew strained over misunderstandings, and the tension of spiritual differences. We ended up not talking to each other for nineteen years.

I began to feel the Lord call me out of my past. Just like He called Abraham. Genesis 12:1-3 says, "The Lord had said to Abram, 'Go from your country, your people, and your father's household to the land I will show you. I will make you into a great nation, and I will bless you; I will make your name great, and you will be a blessing. I will bless those who bless you, and whoever curses you I will curse; and all peoples on earth will be blessed through you.'"

God was calling me to leave what was familiar and walk forward in faith. It wasn't easy; it was painful. But it was necessary. Luke 9:60 says, "Jesus said to him, 'Let the dead bury their own dead, but you go and preach the kingdom of God.'"

I could not walk with people who didn't believe, even people I loved, and with Christ at the same time.

The roads had split, and I chose mine. I chose Him.

But I wasn't completely on my own. God sent people into my life, Christians who discipled me, encouraged me, and helped me grow. I learned about grace, forgiveness, and the love of God in ways I had never known before.

Also exciting, I began feeling the stirrings of a deeper purpose. Maybe my story, my journey, wasn't just for me. Maybe I was called to share it.

On my return flights to Tel Aviv, I would share my testimony every chance I got. I couldn't keep quiet about Jesus—Yeshua. My heart overflowed with joy, hope, and truth.

Some of those experiences were incredibly moving and powerful. One time, a Hebrew-speaking flight attendant I knew asked me the same question I had asked my roommate. "How do you know Jesus is the Son of God?"

I said, "Well, just ask God. Ask Him if He has a son." And so on that plane, thirty thousand feet in the air, I held her hand on the jump seat while she prayed, "Yeshua, if you're real, let me know. I want to know."

After the flight, she and her boyfriend, now husband, found they had a last-minute room change at the beautiful hotel in Tel Aviv where we crew members used to stay. When they saw what was laid out for them, they called me screaming. "You've got to come here. Did you do this?"

I ran to the room, and the room had, waiting for them, bread and a bottle of wine with a corkscrew in the shape of the cross. I knew people would say, "Oh, that's just bread and wine." But no, we had just prayed that God would show Himself.

Even though God answered that prayer and showed Himself to the flight attendant and her boyfriend, I don't think they accepted him, at least not then. You really have to pay attention to those moments because the Holy Spirit is so gentle, and He will show up. Don't blow Him off. He will talk to you if you seek Him.

While the Israeli flight attendant in that story was at least open to a conversation about God, that was not what I typically experienced when sharing the gospel. In most cases, I was met with confusion and judgment.

One day, during a flight, an angry customer caught my attention. Wanting to bring him peace, I gave him a gospel tract. I thought I was doing a kind thing, but he became enraged. He threatened to sue the airline. Not long after, I was summoned to a serious meeting with my supervisor. I knew what was coming.

They wanted to fly me to Newark for a disciplinary review, but I feared I would be stranded with no way home. So I stayed in Houston, ignored the meeting, and eventually received the letter: I had been let go.

I had lost my wings—but I had gained heaven.

Still, the situation didn't look good. Not at first. I had no college degree. English wasn't my first language. I had no money, just my roommate and her mom who supported me in prayer and faith. Even her dad and sweet special needs brother treated me like family. They took me in with love, adopting me as their spiritual daughter and sister.

I started over as a minimum-wage fashion stylist for a clothing retailer. Slowly but surely, I worked my way up: sales lead, co-manager, store manager, then multi-unit store manager. God opened doors.

I moved on my own, living in a nice apartment, driving a BMW, owning a Louis Vuitton—and managing luxury retail stores. I looked like a success story. As I stepped into leadership, I became serious, hard-working, and deeply responsible. But my heart still whispered this wasn't the full calling.

I continued to feel tension between two worlds: the desire for fame and the call to ministry. As a child, I dreamed of acting. As a teen, I wanted to be seen and known. So I took new headshots and eventually joined an acting agency and started auditioning again.

At the same time, I still witnessed about Jesus and read His Word daily. This pattern continued for about a decade.

I had a high calling on my life to serve the Lord, and I was fine with being single. But then, when I was in my thirties, I started rethinking my decision not to pursue marriage. I wanted someone in my life.

I started dating. It was hard finding someone, especially when I was working all the time, but I finally met a nice guy, the man I would marry. We connected right away because I felt like he understood me.

When we met, I thought he was the coolest guy in the world. He drove a yellow Lamborghini and brought yellow flowers to our first date. He's eighteen years older than I (I was thirty-seven; he was fifty-five), but he didn't act his age.

I couldn't figure him out. He's older on one hand, but he was riding a skateboard, playing guitar, and driving like a race car driver. He had a Porsche and a Lamborghini. His son had an orange Jaguar that his father had bought for his sixteenth birthday.

They were this cool duo, father and son, who loved cool cars and having fun.

I loved this man right away, but at first, I didn't think he was the one for me. Surely God was going to send me a Godly man, maybe a preacher. And this guy wasn't any of that. He was more worldly. He was about business and cars, and mostly, all about his son.

Honestly, it was his teenage son at that time who helped win me over and opened my heart to wanting a relationship with his dad. He was so handsome and polite and smart and mature for his age. And this young man grew up as an only child, so he reminded me of myself. The two of them together, they were adorable. I knew it was a package deal, that I got two for the price of one, and I embraced them both. Today, he is my bonus son—the same age as the son I would have had twenty-five years ago. God truly has a way of restoring what the enemy tried to steal.

Not that everything came together right away. I had to build a relationship with this confident, charming man. We had to build trust slowly, through time, conversations, and care.

Finally, we moved to Florida together—his condo, my dream setting. Palm trees, ocean breezes, and a new chapter. But while I was happy, I knew something was missing. We weren't married yet. And deep down, I knew I wasn't fully surrendered to God. I remembered those early days when the Holy Spirit would visit me so powerfully. I had experienced visions, dreams, and peace like a river. That fire had dimmed. But God hadn't moved—I had. And He was calling me back.

At the same time, God was paving the way for restored relationships with my family. My partner had lost his parents. One day, he encouraged me to reconnect with my mother. "If I could see my parents again," he said, "I'd do anything."

His words pierced me. I restored peace with my mom. I reconnected with Israel. And eventually, my partner and I got married.

My spirit felt lighter than it had in years.

CHAPTER 14

THE RETURN TO MY CALLING

After marriage, a shift happened. I was back in alignment with the Lord. The pattern of sin was gone. The peace returned. I began to write sermons. I started preparing again for the ministry I had once paused.

Even while working retail, I would see visions of myself on stage, preaching to multitudes in faraway lands. I wanted to warn people about hell because I knew it was real. I didn't want anyone to go there. My heart beat for the lost. It still does.

And God, who'd once prepared my heart to accept His truth, was now preparing me for a ministry. In Florida, I managed retail stores for a while and then began managing a medical spa, which led to organizing special events for them. After getting married, I started working for my husband, but God put the idea of using my experience with the spa to launch an event company.

My first event was a collaboration with the medical spa I'd worked with, and it was a hit. The idea was to focus on women's spiritual and physical health. That was a success, which inspired the idea for a ministry focused on hosting faith-based community events. I still longed to get on stage and preach. Now, it felt like God was telling me that I didn't need a church to discover me to share His truth. I could use my own microphone.

On January 17, 2025, when I hosted our first community faith event, I grabbed the mic and shared my testimony. God had this in mind all along. Even the date of our event was significant. A while back, I had introduced myself to a pastor who was preaching on the beach near our Florida home.

I'd noticed his church services in the past and could feel the Holy Spirit working. So I approached after a service and asked the pastor for a blessing. He told me I had the spirit of Daniel and that I would be used by the Lord to lead others to Him. Daniel 1:17 came to mind, a scripture I used to quote: "As for these four young men, God gave them knowledge and skill in all literature and wisdom; and Daniel had understanding in all visions and dreams."

Now, with our new faith-based event ministry, I'd be in a position to be a light, just like Daniel.

I still have a passion for film and creativity, and I'm going to use it, but I'm going to use it for God and for ministry, not for my glory. My ministry cannot be the Cheri show; it has to be about Jesus.

And above all, we must be sharing the good news that Jesus is the Messiah.

Life is short. God told us our life is like a vapor. So it's so important to tell people: There's only one criterion to make it to heaven, and that's receiving the sacrifice Jesus made on the cross.

"For God so loved the world that He gave His only begotten Son, that whoever believes in Him should not perish but have everlasting life" (John 3:16). That's the scripture that echoes through my ministry. I want to create events and share my story, ultimately, so people will seek God for themselves and find Him.

I hope my story encourages those who hear it.

I wasn't looking for religion. I was looking for a Father. And I found Him.

THE END IS STILL UNWRITTEN

Today, I'm happily married and fulfilled. My relationship with my mom is restored.

And much more recently, the door opened a bit to communicate with my father. The conversation began with my dad's cousin from England, who spoke with Dad and then texted me what he said.

"He recalled how close he was to you before the marriage with your mother finally broke up. He said he could not accept you back if you lived as a Christian. But he agreed to give you a chance to explain to him personally."

In my response text, sent via Dad's cousin, I poured out my heart to "my dedy." I told him I loved him. I shared the hurts I'd experienced since he left. I told him I forgave him. And then, in detail, I shared my testimony with him, from coming to the U.S. to work as a flight attendant at age twenty-one to how God gave me new life after I cried out to Him in the bathroom. I told him about the three hundred Messianic prophecies that Jesus fulfills.

And I begged my father to pray to God Himself and ask Him sincerely if He has a son.

Dedy, I will always love you. Your daughter is a born-again believer and I will never reject the Messiah who died for me. He comes first. My faith is burning in my bones. This is real for me! It is my passion. My heart, my life, and my salvation is Yeshua, my Messiah. He and Yehova are one! Elohim is plural. . . Just like you're a father, a son, and a husband, He is Aba, and son, and ruach hakodesh.

While I haven't seen any evidence that my dad asked God if He has a son, he didn't use the truth I poured out to him as an excuse to once again close the door to our relationship. Our cousin followed up to tell me my dad didn't think it would be necessary for me to renounce my beliefs before we meet in person.

I'm more hopeful about our relationship than I have been in years, even though it's challenging, since most of his children and grandchildren don't even know I exist. I'm grateful I had the chance to communicate with my dad openly from my heart.

So what's next?

My mission is clear now: to evangelize the world. To share the truth that Jesus is real, that He loves us, and that He offers hope—beyond this life and into eternity.

This may be the end of this book, but it is not the end of my story. With Christ, there is no end, only everlasting life.

And my prayer for you, dear reader, is simple: Call upon His name. Seek Him with all your heart.

And you will find Him—just like I did.

Prayer of Salvation

Dear God,

I come to You in the Name of Jesus (Yeshua). I admit that I am not right with You, and I want to be right with You. I ask You to forgive me of all my sins.

The Bible says if I confess with my mouth that "Jesus (Yeshua) is Lord" and believe in my heart that God raised Him from the dead, I will be saved (Rom. 10:9).

I believe with my heart and confess with my mouth that Jesus (Yeshua) is the Lord and Savior of my life. Thank You for saving me! In Jesus' (Yeshua's) Name I pray. Amen.

John 3:3

"Jesus answered and said to him, 'Most assuredly, I say to you, unless one is born again, he cannot see the kingdom of God."

SCRIPTURE REFERENCES

Messianic prophesies

Isaiah 7:14

"Therefore the Lord Himself will give you a sign: Behold, the virgin shall conceive and bear a Son, and shall call His name Immanuel."

Micah 5:2

"But you, Bethlehem Ephrathah, though you are little among the thousands of Judah, yet out of you shall come forth to Me the One to be Ruler in Israel, whose goings forth are from of old, from everlasting."

Psalms 2: 7-8

"I will declare the decree: The Lord has said to Me, 'You are My Son, today I have begotten You. Ask of Me, and I will give You the nations for Your inheritance, and the ends of the earth for Your possession.'"

Psalms 22:16

"For dogs have surrounded Me; the congregation of the wicked has enclosed Me. They pierced My hands and My feet."

Proverbs 30:4

"Who has ascended into heaven, or descended?

Who has gathered the wind in His fists?

Who has bound the waters in a garment?

Who has established all the ends of the earth?

What is His name, and what is His Son's name,

If you know?"

Healing scriptures

1 Peter 2:24

"Who Himself bore our sins in His own body on the tree, that we, having died to sins, might live for righteousness—by whose stripes you were healed."

Galatians 3:13

"Christ has redeemed us from the curse of the law, having become a curse for us (for it is written, 'Cursed is everyone who hangs on a tree')."

John 10:10

"The thief does not come except to steal, and to kill, and to destroy. I have come that they may have life, and that they may have it more abundantly."

Prosperity scriptures

Luke 6:38

"Give, and it will be given to you: good measure, pressed down, shaken together, and running over will be put into your bosom. For with the same measure that you use, it will be measured back to you."

Malachi 3:10

"'Bring all the tithes into the storehouse, that there may be food in My house, and try Me now in this,' says the Lord of hosts, 'If I will not open for you the windows of heaven and pour out for you such blessing that there will not be room enough to receive it.'"

Faith scriptures

Mark 11:24

"Therefore I say to you, whatever things you ask when you pray, believe that you receive them, and you will have them."

Hebrews 11:1

"Now faith is the substance of things hoped for, the evidence of things not seen."

Hebrews 11:6

"But without faith it is impossible to please Him, for he who comes to God must believe that He is, and that He is a rewarder of those who diligently seek Him."

Romans 10:17

"So then faith comes by hearing, and hearing by the word of God."

Love scriptures

1 John 4:8

"He who does not love does not know God, for God is love."

John 13:34

"A new commandment I give to you, that you love one another; as I have loved you, that you also love one another."

Matthew 6:15

"But if you do not forgive men their trespasses, neither will your Father forgive your trespasses."

1 Corinthians 13

1 Though I speak with the tongues of men and of angels, but have not love, I have become sounding brass or a clanging cymbal.

2 And though I have the gift of prophecy, and understand all mysteries and all knowledge, and though I have all faith, so that I could remove mountains, but have not love, I am nothing.

3 And though I bestow all my goods to feed the poor, and though I give my body to be burned, but have not love, it profits me nothing.

4 Love suffers long and is kind; love does not envy; love does not parade itself, is not puffed up;

5 does not behave rudely, does not seek its own, is not provoked, thinks no evil;

6 does not rejoice in iniquity, but rejoices in the truth;

7 bears all things, believes all things, hopes all things, endures all things.

8 Love never fails. But whether there are prophecies, they will fail; whether there are tongues, they will cease; whether there is knowledge, it will vanish away.

9 For we know in part and we prophesy in part.

10 But when that which is perfect has come, then that which is in part will be done away.

11 When I was a child, I spoke as a child, I understood as a child, I thought as a child; but when I became a man, I put away childish things.

12 For now we see in a mirror, dimly, but then face to face. Now I know in part, but then I shall know just as I also am known.

13 And now abide faith, hope, love, these three; but the greatest of these is love.

PHOTO ALBUM

Grandpa visits Dad on the battlefield, Yom Kippur War, 1973.

Daddy's graduation.

Us three! Me and my best friends—my parents.

Little me on my fourth birthday.

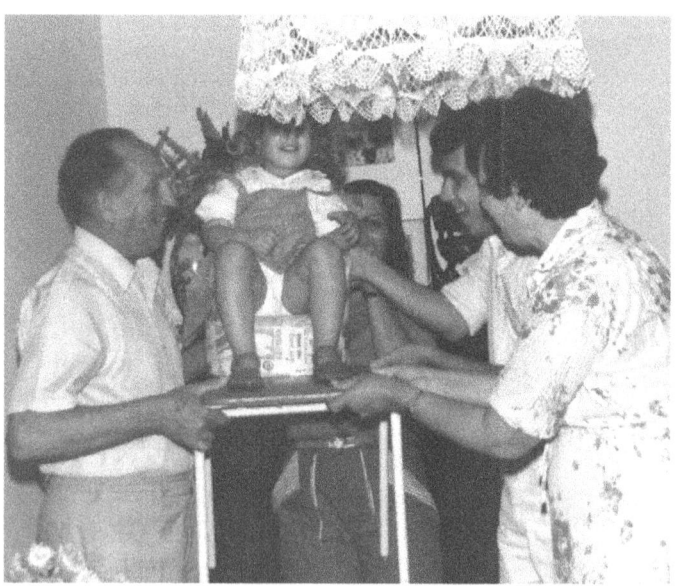

Birthdays were everything.

Happy days, playing with my mom.

Daddy's girl, the apple of his eye.

My forever Mommy and Daddy — my forever prayer: that you'll know the Lord: "As for me and my house, we will serve the Lord" (Joshua 24:15).

My very first headshots.
Sweet sixteen and chasing my dream.

The bread and the wine with a cross-shaped cork screw.

Dad as an Orthodox Jew.

Boss in red heels, in luxury retail, with a '30s vibe.

Early 40s headshot, giving acting one more chance.

Still crushing on my husband, Matt, like it's day one.

About the Author

Cheri Ben-Dov Williams is a motivational faith speaker and founder of Dove Ministry. She is an Israeli-American whose life was radically transformed through a personal revelation of Jesus Christ, the Messiah—revealed to her through the Messianic prophecies, the Hebrew Word of God, and the richness of the Hebrew language. Compelled by the call of God, Cheri is passionate about proclaiming the good news of salvation to all who hunger for truth.

Her calling is to fulfill the Great Commission—sharing Christ with the world and boldly preaching the Word of God as the final authority. She teaches the Word of Faith as God's remedy for every human need, declaring that God's Word is the answer, and Jesus is the Word made flesh.

Cheri is an ordained minister and a graduate of Lakewood Church's internship program (2007), where she served as a youth ministry leader. She also studied at Rhema Correspondence Bible School and continues to grow through the teachings of Kenneth E. Hagin.

ABOUT DOVE MINISTRY

We are a nonprofit ministry dedicated to hosting faith-based events, founded by Cheri Ben-Dov Williams. Through her powerful testimony, books, and short films, we share God's love and healing with all who seek truth and restoration.

For speaking engagements or to learn more, visit www.doveministryfl.com.

Call:
1 (844) 777-DOVE
1 (844) 777-3683

Write:
2637 East Atlantic Boulevard #1073
Pompano Beach, Florida 33062